Praise for
BURY THE SEED

"This is feminine wisdom at its most luminous – radically accessible, urgently sensual, clear as snowmelt and grounded as a grandmother oak. Goddess save us from another self-important self-help book. Brooke McNamara's poetry is a bell: wake up; give thanks; leave nothing out."

MIRABAI STARR,
Author of *Wild Mercy*
and *Caravan of No Despair*

"*Bury the Seed* has become my new secret little pleasure that I gleefully pull out while in the line at the market, sitting in my dentist's office or while waiting for the light to change. I can't get enough of this delightfully refreshing reset of my mood and mindset. Every once in a while, a prophet appears in the form of a poet. I'm happy to say that Brooke McNamara is our most recent one. More please!"

KATHERINE WOODWARD THOMAS,
New York Times Bestselling Author
of *Calling in "The One"* and *Conscious Uncoupling*

"These are gloriously urgent wake-up poems — wake up, astonished, to the only moment we have — this moment! McNamara is a modern Zorba. She urges us to stop, to rest, to listen to the life pouring through and over us, to steep ourselves in the mystery that we are."

ROGER HOUSDEN,
Author of *10 Poems to Change Your Life,
Dancing with Joy,* and *Risking Everything*

"Reading Brooke McNamara is like being pulled deliberately, ruthlessly through the eye of the needle. This poetry is refuge. There is no protection from our luminous poverty, nowhere to hide from our belonging to everything. Only our tenderness can pass."

VERA DE CHALAMBERT,
Interspiritual Theologian,
Author of *Kali Takes America*

"Before beginning to read Brooke McNamara's second book of poetry, *Bury the Seed,* light a candle and wrap yourself in a hand knit heirloom blanket. Sip your coffee. Sit in practice for a while, just long enough to prepare yourself for 'cataclysmic knowing,' a figure/ ground shift of your being.

From the first poem to the last, McNamara evokes through her contemplations a spirit of humility, of the ground from which true reverence is born, and which opens the heart to receive all the varied resonances stirred by her words. She follows the path of gravity and descent, in Greek, *kenosis,* the emptying of the self which leads to *katabasis,* the passage down to the roots and foundations of all things. Brooke helps us recognize that this is the place of emptiness from which all possibility and renewal arises."

REV. DAVID C. MCCALLUM, S.J.
VP for Mission Integration and Development,
Le Moyne College

"These poems touch tender places in me and freshly, playfully nudge whatever it is that awakens, astonished, into radical freedom. They evoke so many so-funky so-ordinary moments, illuminating the sacred, utterly miraculous Wonder in which I notice I am always already sitting as I read them."

TERRY PATTEN,
Author of *A New Republic of the Heart,*
Integral Life Practice

"Raw, illuminating, brave, sensual, and highly addictive."

JAMIE CATTO,
Author of *Insanely Gifted,*
Director of *1 Giant Leap* and *Becoming Nobody*

"What a gift it is to see the world through Brooke McNamara's eyes. Her lens is a kaleidoscope of timeless presence, modern motherhood, and the alternating sharp-soft experience of being a woman who tells the truth. Sewn out of the heartbreakingly poignant moments of everyday life, Brooke's poems remind us of our birthright: to notice, in each moment, the aching truth of what it means to be a human being."

KELLY NOTARAS,
Author of *The Book You Were Born to Write*

"Brooke's poems act to awaken this Supreme Identity— the unity of You and Divine Spirit Itself — releasing the novel capacity of your own deepest Creativity. And this Kosmic vitality is what poetry at its best is meant to evoke, calling us to remember the radiant glory that is our own eternal soul. This is what Brooke does for us, for which we can all be truly, deeply grateful."

KEN WILBER,
Author of *Grace and Grit*,
A Brief History of Everything, and *Integral Meditation*

"*Bury the Seed* asks us to 'co-listen,' to attend *with* — we watch grief hatching into newness in these poems and feel the resonance of wonder in our own suffering. These poems change us."

JANET STONE,
Global Yoga Warrior

"What poetry does best is take the slack out of language. It provides spaces for breathing into unspoken truths. Brooke McNamara's poems are taut distillations. They take us beyond the mind into an evanescent encounter with embodied feelings and truths we recognize as borne from the bitter and glorious experience of living. She embraces and invites us towards the immanent in all of its mystery, contradiction, and sensate hunger. Like a spiraling and furious heartbeat, she captures a pulse that endures. She writes deeply from experience and does not shy away from the splendid or the painful. Reading these poems is like sipping a savory winter broth, borne from ingredients that pushed their way through the hardscrabble earth and into an alchemy of transformation through the culinary imagination of a master chef. The poems reek of survival and of nourishment. They are pungent and necessary."

RAY ELIOT SCHWARTZ,
Somatic Movement Educator,
Dance Artist and Activist

"These are poems perfect for sharing aloud, with lovers and loved ones, for gatherings or rituals — but they're also meditative, perfect for moments of self-love and glimpsing the mystery of life."

DAVE ROCK,
Poet, Spoken Word Artist, Storyteller

"Jet lagged and exhausted, my daughter had just fallen asleep next to me as I laid in bed reading Brooke's poems. When I came to the last line of her poem *PRACTICE*, I burst into tears. In that moment, all boundaries vanished between reader and writer, life and death, struggle and liberation. In that moment, I felt her and felt deeply known by her.

The journey of parenting, of pain, and of realization is reflected in Brooke's writing with a simple and undeniable elegance. Brooke's poetry weaves *fire into fabric* and spirit into matter as she pours her heart and transmission through her words. This book is a gift to all of us. May her poetic blessings spread far and wide for the benefit of all."

DUSTIN DIPERNA,
Author of *Streams of Wisdom*

"Edgy, elegant, simple, sacred, and relentlessly real, *Bury the Seed* will stir in you the desire to live a more Awake life. Each poem is a gift, holding moments touched with deep presence, reverence, and wisdom. Thank you, Brooke, for capturing life's raw beauty in the way you uniquely do."

SARA AVANT STOVER,
Bestselling Author of
The Way of the Happy Woman and *The Book of SHE*

"*Can I read you a poem?* I ask my husband. Midway through, I'm crying, struggling to get the words out. I look at him wordlessly through shining eyes, hoping he gets the transmission.

Something has reached out from the page and grabbed my heart so fiercely that I can't speak.

Brooke's words have taken me to another place in consciousness, far from the rocking chair, the cat, and the fire.

So good, my husband says, interrupting my reverie.

Yes, I smile as I return to the room and meet his eyes with mine.

Can I read you another poem? I whisper, full of hope and a little shy about asking.

Not yet, he replies. *Her poems are so rich. It's best to digest them one at a time.*

True, that. Brooke's poems are so rich. So deep in their spiritual realization. So full of everyday Life. It really is best to digest them one at a time.

If you can't help yourself and gulp down the entire collection in one sitting, like I did, I recommend going back again later, like I did. Savor them one at a time... Slowly. Enjoy!"

ALLISON CONTE,
Founder, *Sophia Leadership,*
Instructor, *Harvard Business Publishing,*
and Co-Author of *The New Feminine Evolutionary*

"She had me at the subhead: *poems for releasing more life into you*. With this new collection, Brooke McNamara delivers on that promise. I finish it awake to more of what this life is and can be. It's a marvelous thing, what words can transmit in the hands of a poet as fine as Brooke."

JEFF SALZMAN,
Host of *The Daily Evolver*

"The elegance of her lyrical lines confront us with the contrariness of being, making it possible to tolerate, and yes, perhaps, to even fall into the eye of awakening through the artful unearthing of unity."

TERRI O'FALLON,
Creator of STAGES Model of Human Development

"Brooke McNamara's words fall like raindrops filled with light — fresh, gentle, nourishing, and utterly authentic. They invite us to wake up to the infinite beauty of BEING here and now, completely human and completely divine."

DOROTHY HUNT,
Spiritual Director of Moon Mountain Sangha,
Author of *Only This!*, *Leaves from Moon Mountain*,
and *Ending the Search: From Spiritual Ambition to the Heart of Awareness*

"Brooke's poetry has a quality that consistently causes me to stop, pause, breathe, and both see and feel the present moment (including myself in it) freshly. *Bury the Seed* is such a gift and I am grateful!"

KENDRA CUNOV,
Teacher, Coach, Founder of *The Collective: A Global Web of Women Devoted to Embodied Wholeness*

"Brooke's poetry is dangerously beautiful. Really it shouldn't be read by anyone not willing to be seduced and to really feel themselves. Don't read her work unless you're prepared to be human."

MARK WALSH,
Founder of *Embodied Facilitator Course*,
Author of *Embodiment: Moving Beyond Mindfulness*

"*Bury the Seed* both inspires and provokes. While reading these poems I am equally drawn into an inner-silence, my own inherent divinity, and driven to go deeper in my practice as a poet and meditator. There are also poems rooted in the domestic, in the family, in the daily fact of being human. This is a dynamic book well-suited to the complicated age we live in."

JOSEPH MASSEY,
Author of *A New Silence*

"*Bury the Seed* points to the mystery of life and calls us into a deep relationship with all of it. Brooke's way of drawing us into laughter and tears reveals a way of feminine embodiment that is vivid and appealing. This book is for any spiritual practitioner aiming for Self discovery."

EMILY HORN,
Dharma and Meditation Teacher

"Brooke's voice rises silently and rings through her words, finding a deep well within you. Her words fall far down, creating currents that linger. Brooke's poems weave and reveal the beautiful stories about the inside of all of us. She dares to welcome all the corners - the known and barely glimpsed, and equally the unknown, the hidden and the cauterized. I say yes to the ten thousand secret invitations in Brooke's little big book of poems, calling me to everything."

BEENA SHARMA,
President of the *Vertical Development Academy*

"Brooke McNamara's poems help me breathe. They remind me to feel more deeply, notice more acutely and listen with more profound attention. They remind me that being alive in a body is at once as sacred and miraculous, as it is ordinary, complex and of the earth. Emotionally, somatically and spiritually literate, these works - like all great art - grow with me through time."

RACHEL BLACKMAN,
Theater Artist,
Somatic Educator and Creativity Mentor

"I loved these poems! I read them together with my baby daughter, in the dark of the early morning. They did what for me great poems should do, they stirred something half unknown deep inside, they tenderized me, they transformed me. I read and saw the world and my daughter differently, the everyday veneer of life was stripped back and the deeper, the poetic, was revealed."

JOEL MONK,
Co-Founder of *Coaches Rising*,
Coach, Trainer, and Entrepreneur

"Brooke's poems beautifully articulated in BURY THE SEED are both romantic and mundane, psychological and spiritual, practical and abstract. They are gross and subtle, ordinary and non-ordinary at the same time. They unite the opposites, offering us the atmosphere of radical honesty and intimate insight into Brooke's sacred interior."

Bence Ganti,
Integral Psychologist,
Founder of *Integral Academy*,
Founder of the *Integral European Conferences*

BURY THE SEED

BURY THE SEED
poems for releasing more life into you

Brooke McNamara
Foreword by Alfred K. LaMotte

PERFORMANCE
INTEGRAL
Boulder, Colorado

All Rights Reserved
Copyright © 2020 Brooke McNamara

Performance Integral Edition
Copyright © 2020

No part of this book may be reproduced or transmitted in any form or by any means, electronic or mechanical, including photocopying, recording, or by any other information storage and retrieval system, without permission in writing from the copyright owner.

Published by Performance Integral, Boulder, Colorado.
www.PerformanceIntegral.com
www.BrookeMcNamara.com

FIRST EDITION

2 4 6 8 10 9 7 5 3 1

Cover Design by Alex Musat. www.alexmusat.com/portfolio
Cover Photo by Jewel Afflerbaugh. www.essencesessions.com
Back Cover Photo by Jewel Afflerbaugh.

LIBRARY OF CONGRESS CATALOGING-IN-PUBLICATION DATA

McNamara, Brooke J.   1981 -
  Bury the Seed, poems for releasing more life into you / Brooke McNamara

ISBN-10: 0988768976
ISBN-13: 978-0-9887689-7-0

1. Poetry—General. 2. Poetry—Women Authors. 3. Body, Mind & Spirit—Mindfulness.
4. I.Title.

Library of Congress Control Number: Pending

For Rob,
king of my heart

and

Kanzeon Bodhisattva,
who hears the cries of our world

CONTENTS

Foreword by Alfred K. LaMotte   25
Food and Water   27

Part One: BURY

Funeral for a Future   31
Eleven Endings   33
Failure Poem   35
Marry the Dirt   37
33 Things to do Instead
 of Worshipping Your Phone   38
Conception   41
What Love Is   43
Bury the Seed   45

Part Two: TEND

Practice   49
Prelude   51
Upon Learning Donald Trump
 has been Elected POTUS, I Clean the House   52
What We Make When We're Willing to Praise   53
Small Ones, Silent Ones   54
In the Ring   55
Consecrate   56
Mammal   58
Instructions to the Mother-Writer   60
Service   61
Currency   62
Élan Vital   64
Vow   65
Reunion   66

Part Three: HARVEST

To the Ancient One   71
Caught Kissing   73
No Wisdom   76
Möbius Loop   78
Cacophony at Dawn   79
Voyagers   80
Present   82
Cure   83
Poetry Date   84
Shikantaza   86
Ripeness   87
Falling   88
Sawa   90

Part Four: RELEASE

Break   95
Drop   97
Blessed by the Weight of a Promise   98
Like Stealing a Bone from a Dog   100
When We Were Old   102
Human / Being   104
The Weight of Them   105
Swoon   107
Sovereign   108
Low Down Now   110
Faithful Following the Flow   111
Harmony Playground   112
Chautauqua, Mid-April   113
I Want that Goose to be a Tree   114

Acknowledgements 119
About the Author 123
Resources 125
Notes 127

"The temple bell stops,
but the sound keeps coming
out of the flowers."

~ Bashō

FOREWORD

Brooke's poems are sacred stories of the ordinary. But unlike stories of the past, they are stories of Presence. They make me more awake, right where I Am.

Awake to what? The immanent transcendence of the commonplace, "the guest bed like a love letter... roses on the table... citrus soap by the sink." Brooke's poems help me remember my "ancient promise to love whatever world I wake up in."

Yes, Brooke is a spiritual teacher. Her poems are full of instruction, even the wisdom of her Native American ancestors, as in the poem, *Sawa*, about her Miwok distant relative: "Something untouchable is always there, never not holding you."

Yet her instruction does not come out of the void. Its ground can be that smell of morning coffee, or the layer of children's lunches stuck in the garbage dispose-all. Her soul is not merely within, it is the very tread on the bottom of her little boy's sneaker.

Brooke's poems open the mysteries of initiation in moments of daily living. A young mother recounts her rapture in the liminal sweet confusion between love-making and breast-feeding.

The poet on the toilet reads her favorite book of verse out loud, while nursing her baby in the other arm, when the doorbell rings. This too can be a mindfulness bell: this too is sitting zazen.

A young wife is "caught kissing" in an elevator in Budapest. Who is she kissing? Merely her husband. Yet even here, the iridescent rush of an erotic sacrament. The old Hungarians who catch them at it wink, pronouncing their blessing in thick accents like a chorus of guardian spirits: "It's OK, life is beautiful."

Brooke McNamara poems are not just pieces of literature, they are *useful tools*. Use them to help you "fall into your own bones," where you belong. Use them to encounter "the silver flash of knowing prior to analysis." Use them to find "the hole in you that leads to God."

I hope you might return to these poems again and again, and *use* them. To re-mind yourself. To remind yourself that wherever you are, even as things fall apart, when the center cannot hold, even here the commonplace becomes a sacred space, because your heart is purely engaged in this moment. Now your life, like hers, can "sing songs too original to understand."

~Alfred K. LaMotte

Author of
> *Wounded Bud*
> and *Savor Eternity One Moment At A Time*

> Amazon Author Page:
> amazon.com/author/alfredlamotte

FOOD AND WATER

Sit yourself kindly down
and begin to breathe

with and *as*
the ache of being,
instead of above it.

Remember your first questions.

Enduring and unanswerable,
they can make you
curiosity again.

Gently,

allow your heart to hand you
every last piece
of who you truly are.

This is the food you've been hungry for.

This is the water that will quench.

Softly you dissolve
into an undomesticated friendship
with your world.

Enter into it again
with that quiet quivering
in your now more-human heart,

and let an uncaused joy
come out of your eyes —
so the others feel it,

so it's all of ours
to eat and drink and share.

Part One:

BURY

FUNERAL FOR A FUTURE

I held a funeral for a future
I had always thought was coming,
and buried the world's face as yet.

The silence then
turned me so tiny
the only way forward was to dream
downward

to an early day on earth
before a single heart beat.
The atmosphere filled
with an abiding, cataclysmic knowing —

that if everything
could be born,

every
thing
could
be
born.

Love promises no less.

But a future is gone now.

All we are is this.

Our way could be
to fall toward the medicine
seeded right inside
the untamable, fertile grief
remaking things.

ELEVEN ENDINGS

How do you know right now
that you're alive?
Already the thunder storm is passing
and rivulets of rainwater flow
toward lower ground.

I'm writing this
so I have something to say
as lower down we share ripe silence
and I study the honesty
in how you move.

I love your soft alertness
when you don't know what I'll say,
when I name the little river still moving
along the sidewalk to the graveyard
and the small swamp. I love

how I can't remember if it's you
who started this, or me,
but we're in it now, co-listening,
watching the water trickle down
among the roots of the old elms.

I love not knowing if this is small talk
or big, or where any of it will go.

Already my life has had eleven endings.
I never imagined this could be. Who's the one
alive to write this? I simply do not know.

FAILURE POEM

Let's not let this poem work,
fire it before it begins.

Do not be moved at any turn.

Sit unchanging
at every sound.

Resist
receiving.
Build that brick wall.

Strengthen your antibodies
to any virus of aliveness
desiring your ravishment.

Refuse disruption
of heartbeat, homeostasis,
and current level of wonder or hunger.

In particular allow no agitation
in your upper palate, diaphragm, or pelvic floor.

Let me not whisper a single thing
exciting or frightening along each rib
or in between
each toe.

Inhibit.

Defend against even my soft exhale
at the center of the crown of your head.

Let go
of my hand

and fall back far inside,
far away
from the cacophony of contact.

Tuck yourself away
underneath
even your deepest,
most true self.

And now
let's leave
you here:
hermetically sealed,
utterly
alone.

MARRY THE DIRT

I woke up at 5 to think about the difference
between feral, undomesticated, and insane.

I woke up at 5 to admit some truth.
Fecundity. Appetite. Natural obedience.

I woke up to ask:
Will you come with me?

Will you enter the risk
of every moment embodied

and decaying with me?
You said:

Let's remember the wild art
of never turning back,

to know ourselves
beyond the beyond the beyond.

33 THINGS TO DO INSTEAD OF WORSHIPPING YOUR PHONE

Write a poem called 33 THINGS TO DO
INSTEAD OF WORSHIPPING YOUR PHONE.
Write a poem called PLEASURE
IN THE AFTERNOON.
Worship a faux phone, and make it explicit:
make it huge out of porcelain and put it on an altar,
surrounded by $20 stones with hand-painted words like
"connection," "validation," "self-image,"
"notes to self," "memories," and "how to human."
Throw the real phone to smash the glass
and pick a shard to carve a star
somewhere on your left wrist to scar
and remind you that you can worship your phone
if you want to,
but a glass of water might be more beneficial.
Pay for the groceries you're paying for.
Wait for the bus you're waiting for.
Drive the car you're driving.
Walk across the street.
Duct tape some cut bungee cord to the top and bottom
of your phone and then wear it as an eye patch.
Craft a little winter diorama and stretch 3 cotton balls
around the outside of your phone
to make the snowy frozen lake.
Memorize a 3-minute phone-worship

movement sequence of finger swiping and typing,
and perform it 3 times daily
on your cheek or inner thigh.
Find some pleasure in the afternoon.
Conceive of a sieve subtle and vast enough
to filter out the Benzene from our children's air.
Press one thumb hard into each inner eye dome
until your headache begins to fade.
Grind your phone to a fine powder
and snort some lines —
compare the high to social media likes.
Bury the phone, then dig it up
and use the hole to bury a letter
to Mother Earth asking about her secret longings.
Bury the phone, then dig it up
and use the hole to bury a letter
to Mother Earth asking her forgiveness.
Bury the phone, then dig it up
and use the hole to bury a letter
to your future self with a map
to where the food is stored.
Sit.
Sit till you feel the center of the planet.
Move till you feel the center of yourself.
Shake till you feel the center of yourself
become one with the center of the planet.
Bury yourself, then dig yourself out
and use the hole to hear you say,
"This is my second chance."
Claim this as your only chance.

Use your phone as a platform
to see how long you can balance on one foot.
While balancing, shoot your gaze
to any horizon it can reach.
Hold that horizon with your eyes while still balancing
on one foot on the platform of your phone,
and whisper to it five ways it's different than a screen.
While you're whispering, listen
to the soft sound of your own voice.
While you're listening, notice
the silence inside the sound.
Right when you notice the silence,
curl into a little ball.
To curl correctly, wrap all of yourself tightly
around your own center until you disappear.
Right before you disappear, become
a seed and feed yourself to the future.
Feed yourself to the future
in order to disappear.

CONCEPTION

I know
you're still living
in the bliss
of the Body Original,
here but hidden
in plain sight,

where turquoise
is gold and gold
is steam rising
off the pond at dawn.

When I walk the pond at dawn,
I remember to soften
my gaze
and catch impressions
of you
in the periphery.

You are the sweet peach
ripening in my heart.

You are the humble pearl
brightening in my belly.

You are the little Common Loon

sending your wail
up my spine
to fill my mind
with your location.

And the future's weight
of your life in my arms
has made of my being

a great lighthouse
haunted by longing.

WHAT LOVE IS

for Joyce Bradley, Lloyd Pilatti, and Michael Pilatti

My mom arrived two days after her mom died.
I made the guest bed like a love letter.
I put the picture of grandma on the altar,
roses on the table, citrus soap by the sink.

It was in the fact that she showed up
to help me with the boys
while my husband was away, even in her loss.
It was in the way she made coffee, conversation,
and lego jets with Lundin. It was in the way
her soft hands handled her grandsons.
It was in the fact that she showed up.

I realized: *she's teaching me what love is.*
How we hand ourselves down over decades,
in acts too big, too small, and too many to remember,
riding a force designed to undo us,
fueling the next ones meant to bloom.

Grandma Joyce, I remember the smell of coffee
and your slow smile. Grandpa Lloyd, I remember
picking cherries and you calling me *Blondie*.
Uncle Michael, I remember the koala doll
you gave me and your deep well of kindness.
Where are you now?

What do you know that you couldn't know before?
Are you at rest?

I want to honor you and the pathways you carved,
however bittersweet, for my mom and me and my boys
to have life. Whatever you are now, please teach me
how to love this life before it's over. I feel it dissolving
before I can even write it down.
Teach me how to feel you
winking through the fabric of my daily life,
and pause to breathe you in. Teach me
what this is all about. Please,
teach me what love is.

BURY THE SEED

Pain always teaches me
to make new things.

Less for what the things become
than for how the making
re-makes me
brave and grateful.

Early this morning,
under a cobalt, cloudless sky,
my steps each send instructions
up to worried, humble ears:

The bells are ringing.

It's time you knew —

*in your gripped fist
has always been
your specific
hallowed seed.*

*Release
that lifelong holding
into open hands
and here,*

exactly as you already are,
break ground, dig down,
and simply, faithfully,
bury the seed.

In the moist eternal darkness,
let life split open
and become.

Part Two:
TEND

PRACTICE

Last night I was hoping to make love to my husband
after we got the boys to bed, but instead
we laid down on the couch at 8:45
and fell asleep. I dreamed, then,

that I was dancing in the dark
in my childhood kitchen,
and someone was taking a series of pictures,
adding a filter with a soft red blur.

My husband's dead grandmother,
LaRue Lundin, was there —
more like the atmosphere than anything —
and she was teaching me

that the hardest thing about dying
is trying to say *I love you*
one last time while suffocating.
The only reason I remember this

is because at 10:23 we were blasted awake,
much to my shock and terror,
by a toy dog barking and rolling
around the living room. Why had it turned on,

and why then? Instantly I cried,

because of a mother's exhaustion
mixed with the severity
of receiving LaRue's teaching.

Today, the truth is: I am tired
from the constant service
to my two young boys. I wonder
if I will ever get really good at this.

Part of me wants to just softly sit down,
and crumble. But how will I ever
get those last words out
if I don't practice now?

PRELUDE

Everyone thinks coffee is for drinking.
I put the hot mug in the sweet spot
against the flesh of my sternum
and press the heat into that house of fear.

Oh, my heart!
It's dawn
and I've been called again
by the one who lives beyond the fear.

UPON LEARNING DONALD TRUMP HAS BEEN ELECTED POTUS, I CLEAN THE HOUSE

Mold in the toilets must be scrubbed,
and my toddler's spills demand my supplication.
I always hate the beginning of cleaning,
and the mess gets bigger
before what's under begins to shine.
Some things must be discarded
but the little gifted sailboat mug
will be glued back together for my boy.
Now, head bowed
and crowned with earned beads of sweat,
I'm humming along and my husband
joins my effort. The bad news is:
unearthing, we don't know what we'll find.
The good news is: we don't know what we'll find.
My love, help me lift the weight
of the bed we've been sleeping in
so we can face what's been collecting
under it in the dark. In the corner back there,
I see my lost heirloom ring - ring of my lineage -
has been resting against a dead fly
for who knows how long.

WHAT WE MAKE WHEN WE'RE WILLING TO PRAISE

Ursula Le Guin said,
May your mouth contain the shapes of strange words.[1]

Hafiz,
What we speak becomes the house we live in.[2]

Breathing in, let's pause, and breathing out, praise
what we can of this day,
shaping grief and worry
into oblong and trilateral
exaltations —

even as we might be scared and scarred,
we'll forge ourselves a home to share,

our words a blueprint
for our progeny's inheritance,
an echo of our ancestors'
best intentions.

SMALL ONES, SILENT ONES

Early this morning I woke to my son
standing in my bed, asleep but electric.
"I'm seeing!" he exclaimed, slightly ecstatic,
then crumpled back down to horizontal.

Sometimes sunflowers rise in our dreams.
All soil has eyes, and vision streams
up those leafy columns
toward buttery light above.

Small ones, silent ones,
sometimes we forget
we don't always have to know it all —
show us what we need to see.

IN THE RING

When the story is over,
what will you wish
you'd have said?

Step into the ring,
wakeful.
Find your spine.

CONSECRATE

I know life
is consecrated through me
by a sudden act of declaration,
the capacity to describe reality
but more so envision it.

I know a felt sense
of the wilderness
of potentiality
in love with the very weight
we currently embody.

Our birthright
is to open
within tension
to the upswell and fervor
of what's never yet been,

to bear the load
of not knowing
the next surface or form,
and still keep each other
awake —

to clarify
what it is

we long for most
and then become that
longing,

with all our strength,
and all our surrender,
while it does
with us
what it will.

MAMMAL

Call it ironic or somehow taboo
that just as we near a peak in lovemaking
the sleeping baby somehow knows
and begins to wake,
as if a signal had been sent
from the place of his making,
that non-location where love gazes
into her cauldron of emptiness,
conspiring to bring the next things here to form.

And so tonight,
in the center of our shared radiance,
the pleasure waves stilled in awe
around our cocoon of union, our skin
rippling with heat and light,
our little one calls from across our home.

So I must quickly navigate back
to a different function inside myself,
a different intimacy,
rush across that little divide
from lover to mother
and gather the bundle to my warmth and breast.

However boldly awareness reclaims us as infinite,
the movements of our life are still embedded

in this world of mammal. I nurse Orion
while still tasting the residue of our ecstasy,
bathing in these distinct and various flavors
of how we all love each other
home through flesh and blood.

INSTRUCTIONS
TO THE MOTHER-WRITER

Keep it short.
Tell the truth.
Nothing fancy.

SERVICE

The problem is, I can't write this
without changing.
I plan to work now
and I plan to come back

dawn by dawn
to tend these flowers,
but I don't know
who'll arrive tomorrow:

every time
I serve the garden,
I become the compost.
I become the bloom.

CURRENCY

If you've lost yourself,
or an answer,
just pick a place.

Pick one place
dear to you —
outdoor, indoor, casual, formal —
and go there
once or twice a day.

But every day.
Go.
Sit.
Show up for your place
however you are,

as if it were its day of creation,
spilled out
from some bucket
of undivided light
into specifically this spot —

as if it were its day to die,
the ground about
to split to swallow
every precious detail

without bias or hesitation —

as if it were an old friend,
where you could go at any time
to find suspension
in sweetest tension
between longing and belonging.

Pay this place
your particular attention —
the currency that will unfurl,
one by golden one,
the secrets that are seeking you.

ÉLAN VITAL

I dreamed our world was running out of oxygen.
Oxygen is not quite right. Our world was running out
of that which animates, whatever it is
we live for, whatever it is that's living us, even now.

Lauren and I were sent to find it, mine it, bring it back.
Not a literal excavation, artistic. We set off in the night,
and did not hesitate. The landscape had a sense of thirst
colossal, awful. We set our compass for that breathing
inside of things; we'd go absolutely anywhere
to court and tend it —

Mine
made no more sense.

VOW

My vow
in making poems
is to someday succeed
at stitching fire
into fabric.

REUNION

When I had finally had enough
of my own endless,
uncreative complaints,
I made my promise to do better.

I turned around.

I journeyed backward
for millions of miles
and millions of years
into the end
of miles and years

to retrieve these words
for you:

You must be the one

to do or undo
whatever it takes
to remember and activate
your own
furiously prolific heart,

and your innate allegiance
to every creature living

and dying here with you.

Our whole world is aching

*to be intimate with you
again!*

*Kiss me,
sweet one,
when you make it
home.*

Part Three:
HARVEST

TO THE ANCIENT ONE

After I sent you away
I found your bright
thorn growing
in my throat.

Shocked
by the piercing
when I bent
my head to pray,

I jumped to hunt
the salve
anywhere possible
outside myself.

But last night
by accident
I prayed so strong
it punctured, penetrating

the center, here,
and the holy
serum flowed
from the inside.

Finally, finally,

I know this:
you did not send
the pain to punish

but to beg my head
to bow more deeply
into this flood
of brilliant self-love.

CAUGHT KISSING

In Budapest,
in the Danubius Grand Hotel on Margaret Island,
we just got caught kissing, blocking the elevator door.
I'd been out running, endorphins pumping,
my sweaty hair slicked back, patches of moisture
on my body the evidence of effort. Coming back
to retrieve our boys from their grandparent's care,

I ran right into my husband by surprise,
who'd been working as well
in the hotel conference room, decked out
in his fine attire, the suit he'd married me in
in fact, testosterone-flushed from being in leadership.

Let me tell you —
it was as if it were our first encounter ever,
and at the same time we'd been mates for life
for lifetimes since the earliest life forms on earth
had ever practiced such a thing.

Hey, let's get a room — I said, joking.
Kiss me — he said, not joking.

And he grabbed me there,
to press bellies and breath
and fertile eternities

into each other
without a single thought for narration,

and the violin hymn folded into silence
at all my seams
erupted its call of solemn longing

and all the subtle buds
meditating in my darkness
blossomed their pink peony mouths
perfectly wide open,

and for a moment we fell,
like that,
through all the floors of the world,

and we were held,
like that,
beheld like that,

joined by the presence of an inward force,
found to each other freshly
inside the forgotten light we always are.

Suddenly aware of others around us,
we opened our eyes,
caught in the act.

Sorry! we giggled, and pulled apart,
he to his next meeting,

me to the inside of the decadent elevator
to get back to our babies.

Ascending to the second floor,
the two strangers smiled,
sharing the mischief,
and in a thick, musky Hungarian accent,

It's okay, life is beautiful —
one of them winked.

NO WISDOM

No is also love,
of course.
Sometimes
right action speaks

through a primordial tongue,
silver flash
of knowing
prior to analysis,

before worry has a chance
to thread and congeal
up from gut
to heart and throat.

I don't know
how to know
no is right.
Let's experiment:

taste negation
with every intelligent cell now —
wear your limit daringly
like a prized heirloom and birthright.

Does your body brighten

and ring a little?
Then savor
how *yes* to your *no*

can activate
inborn wisdom,
like the undulating spine
of the dancer transcending.

MÖBIUS LOOP

My holding
him is
holding me.

CACOPHONY AT DAWN

In silence
every thing
reveals
its sacred nature.

In sound,
the silence
says
its secret names.

What are we ever doing
but making traces
of beauty dissolving
out of absolutely nothing at all?

VOYAGERS

I noticed the emphatic nose picking
of my 3-year-old, Lundin, as I read him the lines,

*Space probe Voyager 1 was launched over 30 years ago.
It flew past Jupiter, Saturn, and Saturn's large moon, Titan,
and it's still going. Soon it will leave our Solar System
and disappear into deep space.*[3]

Here's a Kleenex, buddy, I offered.

*It's okay, Mama, I already pushed the booger
back into my nose and soon
it will disappear into deep space,* he said.

Is the deep space inside
as deep as outer space?
Does infinity go in just like it goes out?

Instantly I was captivated by the fantasy
of Voyager 1 and Lundin's booger
simultaneously penetrating deep space
in opposite directions, forever.

Imagining infinity
in any direction
is enough to stop the mind,

so by now I was utterly wonder struck
watching in my mind
this bi-directional probing of emptiness,
this mirroring of macro and micro,
this cosmic duet of Lundin's booger and Voyager 1
voyaging deeper in and out,
beyond forever both ways.

But the deepest secret
I can never tell
is how these two unique vehicles
did not voyage forever apart,
but instead eventually arrived
at opposite sides of the same horizon
where all infinities ultimately meet

in a love too blazing
for our human eyes to survive,
in a beauty so crushing
most of us forget to remember,

and how this place
where Lundin's booger interpenetrates Voyager 1,
where everything intermingles with nothing,

is both far, far away
and at the same time
the exact center
of your very own human heart.

PRESENT

Shaving my legs
in the hot bath,
such startling affection

for the round peak
of my left knee,
I re-remember:

it's not mine to keep.

CURE

Love has plucked
the sickest parts of me
and gathered them

to her whispering lips
to sing songs
too original to understand.

Gentle, transcendent,
piercing, turning,
Her words

have flipped a switch.
From the bowels
of my suffering

She birthed
a pale blue translucent butterfly,
tattooed it on my chest.

It won't stop softly moving
its fragile, indestructible wings.
It won't stop singing our Source.

POETRY DATE

I read recently
that when the great Russian ballet impresario,
Sergei Diaghilev, commissioned a new text
from Jean Cocteau in 1917,
and the poet asked for direction on what to create,
Diaghilev simply said: *Astonish me*.[4]

This morning I'm up early with baby Orion,
tiptoeing to the coffee through the layers of dark
and hungry as usual to start the day with a little poetry.

But I'm groggy, and the baby wants to be held,
and I have to pee, so I imagine my two arms multiplied,
like those glorious images of Kwan Yin,
and then I wield them like so —

holding baby, coffee, and Billy Collins's
Horoscopes for the Dead, I somehow get
my pants down and the toilet seat up,
descend and open the book,

and now we're really cooking —
our own little poetry date is rollicking along
in the dawn light of the bathroom,
and everyone is happy —

a bladder relieved, the coffee awakening,
baby and mama both joyful because we're touching
and he's trying to eat the book,
and I'm reading out loud on the pot
that one about purpose,
and it's ending with:

my true vocation —

*keeping an eye on things
whether they existed or not...*[5]

When the doorbell rings
my pants are around my ankles
and my hands are full

of being astonished, the way
you're supposed to feel
after reading a good poem,
the way this baby feels about just about everything,

the way we both look in the mirror
when I stand
and smooch him all over
and turn around
and really look.

SHIKANTAZA

I don't know what power is rising
but I can feel its longing to take form.

In the crisp dark of pre-dawn
I set out walking to my seat.
Warm wind makes such honest contact
with what skin of me's exposed,
I feel partnered in my endeavor to get there.

There is a home
no words
can reach or conceal,
no fatigue
can keep us from waking for,
no habit
can stain.

Compelled by a faith
that has no object,
we're drawn
to take our seat.

Arriving now,
just sit!
Every time we choose this,
we're chosen
to be home.

RIPENESS

The more our pleasure
flowers forth,

the more the all
of everything

swells open
to bear the fruits

it always everywhere
aches to.

FALLING

This is not a stage
for me to tell you
how to improve
in any way.

There is dignity
in staying with whatever's real
with a long spine bathed in breath,
even as we fall.

If you're still
listening, thank you.
May we turn
from this tiny contact here

toward the opening day grateful,
with gumption,
receiving what we belong to.
Last night I dreamed

a baby cow fell
from a periwinkle sky,
and when I helped him
stand,

the vertebrae under velvet fur

rose and fell like little hills
beneath my happy hand.
I'm telling my young son this dream.

He's laughing sparks
of hilarity out his eyes,
their beauty barely matched
by the softly falling snow outside.

SAWA

It's not always the right thing
or the smartest
or easily done
or even possible

but if it is
and you can feel that
then go ahead
and begin

to let down your guard.

Good. Now can you hear me?
Wherever you are —
in your favorite armchair,
riding a bus downtown,
or waiting for the kettle's call —

can you hear my voice?

I have nothing to give you,
Friend. Nothing
but my favorite story.

I want to give it to your marrow.
Listen:

My mother has native Miwok blood running
through her veins — our roots go deep
in Northern California. I first learned
to formally meditate living in San Francisco
at age twenty-four. Inside my own mind
I found a woman.
She told me clearly her name was *Sawa*.
Though no good at stillness, I found devotion
to her so I went to her every day, inside my mind.
She looked like my mother, but more Miwok:
long brown hair, cream-colored animal skin dress.
Deepest radiance.
She showed me things that were saving my soul.
Her wisdom was soothing,
but surprising: lessons I was getting
from nowhere else. I found her
every day, inside my mind.

Sawa, help me with this sorrow. *Follow me.*
Fill me with vitality. *Follow me.*
Madness is after me. Opening is swallowing me.
Follow me, follow me.
Please, just be with me for a time. *Yes.*
Always there, never not holding me.

I told no one about her, embarrassed
that I had an invisible friend
named Sara who couldn't pronounce her *R*'s.
Six years of this! My secret source of sanity and insight!

Six years, before I learned the origin of her name.
I found her every day, inside my mind.
Age thirty, over late night wine with my sister
I saw a picture in a deck of cards that looked like Sawa
so I finally shared the story.
My sister urged me to research the name, and I found:

SAWA:
Female Native-American Miwok name
meaning stone or boulder.

Can you hear my voice?

Courage, then —
pay attention to what you pray to!
Bow down, and every once in awhile,
give up. We are held by stronger things,
I promise. We are held — if you are willing
to turn backward toward your own soul,
and take one surrendered breath
and one intentional step, you will find
without a doubt that someone is there
for you, something untouchable
is always here,
never not holding you.

Part Four:
RELEASE

BREAK

Rest, now.
Let the weight you run from every day
now draw you down.

Later there will be time to tend
to everything left undone.
Now, rest.

Fall
into your own bones
lying horizontal on this ground.

Come
into your dark corners.
Come into this

original nakedness
under all the layers.
Come where all your losses

split
you
open.

Don't rise,
yet —

rest.

Be drawn deeper down
into the salt tide of tears.
Let grief wash you,

then drown you
beyond the name
you first were given,

when you reached to touch
your own mother's face for the very first time,
and she smiled her light down into you.

Now reach those same fingers
for the face of infinity —
so that, opening your eyes,

you will know
the one dreaming you
is pleased with you,

that everything seen
is your self,
and that now is the time

to rise wholehearted into the work
aching to be animated
by precisely you.

DROP

I forgive myself
so fully
I slip through

the hole in me
that leads to God —
not a him-her-it,

but a whole holding
as I forever
fall.

BLESSED BY THE WEIGHT
OF A PROMISE

Do you remember
falling off
the edge of a thought
into that nameless, endless
viridian lagoon?

Do you remember afterward
how I held you in the liquid
firmly, floating vertically
with our toes dipped one inch
into the bottom's murky sand?

Rippling waters
framed our faces,
whose upward gazing braided
into one force
searching the cosmos.

Do you remember choosing to leave
the waters, allowing air
to dry our skin, goosebumps
signaling our sensitivity to teachings
of a subtle breeze?

And how we both then chose to go

in separate directions
and feel our way through
that novel world,
each alone.

I found layers for warmth
and a smooth stone
to put in my pocket
to remind me:
I am blessed

by the weight of an ancient promise
to love whatever world
I wake up in —
to receive it with sober eyes,
respond with warm hands.

Where are you now?

LIKE STEALING A BONE FROM A DOG

When you're trying to balance on one leg in passé,
you sneak away the hand still holding the barre
so, so slowly, like stealing a bone from a dog,

my teacher taught me at Joffrey ballet camp
when I was eleven. I think of it now as I try
for the third time

to lay down my napping baby without waking him.
These are the secret rites of early motherhood:
we must show up again and again, but sometimes,

like now, we must learn to disappear.
Holding Orion, I gather myself into one piece,
then smooth and empty out, so there are no snags

of a self in me to pull him up from sleep to surface.
But this is a high art. Bending down
over the little bed, his hint of grimace

and tightening body tell me I've failed again.
Stand back up. More bouncing. More humming.
More soothing. More deep breaths.

This time, though, I turn around,

and become suddenly confronted
with the wall of my ancestors.

They see me in my subtle struggle.
Like stealing a bone from a dog, they say.
Bouncing the baby, I greet them: great-grandmother

and namesake, Myrtle Julia, holding my mom as a baby.
Grandma Joyce looking off, distracted. Kenneth Pierce,
Robert Lundin, Alma Vera Lembke Brown.

Thank you, I say.
Thank you, I say again.
They're watching me care for their lineage.

All at once their gazes cohere and amplify:
This! they say.
This is how you disappear! they say.

WHEN WE WERE OLD

When we were old we forgot all the lines of our poems
because we'd become them. When we were old
we remembered all the wanting of the past,
how our hungry bodies had pulsed
for more and more life.
We forgot to wonder what could be better than this,
and instead opened into that silent satisfaction
of having already been fed. When we were old all
the hideous images we'd seen of the human organism
hating itself through some invented other
revealed themselves as the movie of what had been,
but not the real thing at all.

The real thing then revealed itself to us,
when we were old, and warmed our faces
as if around a fire. And we grieved,
and we grieved, and we hatched
from the grieving and became new,
even when we were old. When we were old
we forgot about ever getting to that other
imagined place, and so instead became
the blessing, descending into our very own feet
for the very first time, which were just
the right shape for walking slowly
the golden dirt path each day.

When we were old we took time
to write love letters again,
to the beetle and the bison
and the cumulus cloud,
who remembered us as sacred
so our bellies could finally soften again
and our clenched jaws could release.
When we were old we forgot all the names
of things, and sat and laughed
together until the laughter broke
into blue-black butterflies
that sailed away in the ten directions.

HUMAN / BEING

Why is it difficult to wake up?
Reversing momentum takes effort.

Why is it easy to wake up?
Every thing dissolves except what's already awake.

THE WEIGHT OF THEM

They're getting heavier, my boys,
so my arms are getting more sore, then stronger.
What's the word for "vacation"
when it includes the work of tending all their needs?
While they played in the sand and the sun served up
its final portions of the day, Rob said,
Can you believe their existence is entrusted to us?

I am genuinely wondering how to relax into that fact.

Lundin is four and Orion ten months.
We crossed the Atlantic last Monday and I cried
getting the rental car. I did keep my shit together
in the Caves of Campanet yesterday,
where I took the boys while Rob was working,
and the tight, dim, damp, steep, slippery, low-ceiling'ed
labyrinth awoke an abundance of energy in Lundin,
nap-needing cries and flailing from Orion,
dagger glances from the Latvian tourist group
obviously not impressed with my brood,
and low-blood-sugar, over-heating,
claustrophobic panic in me.

I could go on. It's both a shit-show and a dream
here on vacation with the McNamaras.
But what I really want to say is this:

when Rob was driving us home after dinner last night
and Lundin with his chocolate ice cream cheeks
fell asleep leaning on my shoulder in the backseat,
and then Orion drifted off nursing on my lap,
I could feel the weight of them,
right then, setting me down on earth,
telling my body: *this is where you reside.*
They were holding me, downward,
with their full release, opposite how I hold them.
And it happened again this morning,
sitting on the porch, when Lundin climbed up
on my lap, my body his lounge chair,
and we listened to the tractors and the birds.
With all my spinning ambition pinned, again,
by his thirty-seven pounds, I found my *placefulness*
right here in Campanet — and as I rooted,
I filled from the ground up with a gladness
that liquified and trickled down my cheeks,
dampening his tumble of curls
resting on my chest.

And also - later - I could feel that something,
something like an unseen stream, held the whole
pack of us in our various movements
of the morning, and carried us forward,
where the boys' bodies and their lives
get only bigger, only heavier,
and certainly both darker and brighter,
and press me only more perfectly
into a strength I have yet to embody.

SWOON

Eternity
will always love
urgency.

But urgency must grow up
before she thinks to lie down
with eternity in his warm
and endless night,

and there find
her most radiant face.

SOVEREIGN

You can't have me.
I have woken irreversibly
from the dreamscape
in which I needed your name
to use my voice.

You can't mold me.
I have gazed backward
through the blazing seal
around my own original mind,
and found perennial refuge here.

I have lapped,
sipped, and devoured
the elixir that springs
from my own unborn body
into my phenomenal heart.

You can't touch what I am now.
Now I know the buoyancy
of the perfect curves in my upright spine,
the opulent, round grounding
of my feet flesh on the floor.

Oh, bless you, who thought
you could use and consume me!

My laughter is rolling in your direction
and its windstorm breaks
every bone not yet woken.

LOW DOWN NOW

Stop planning. It's not going to work
this time. There are better ways
to do this and you know it.
Let's take a moment to pause
and imagine pulling the rug
out from under our own feet.
Can you see me - reaching down,
tugging, grunting, crashing
on my own ass? Ridiculous!
But it's good. It's so good
for us to fold, my friend.
Low down now, let's crawl
a quiet, curving way forward
from our guts — let's sniff
for what, if we were wild
again, would feed us,
and feed us
to the whole.

FAITHFUL FOLLOWING THE FLOW

In these moments I let myself thaw
from noun to verb, finding my own
liquidity, and let gravity begin
to pull like an old, sweet summoning,

I then sluice through labyrinthian cracks
in my own becoming, flowing faithfully
right to the feet of this great mountain
of stillness behind my sternum.

And then — here I am
ancient, drunk
on the richness of gaining
absolutely nothing at all.

HARMONY PLAYGROUND

Brooklyn, New York

We sat in the rain watching wet people
leveled by weather to a humorous common ground.
Remember how the clusters of humans
(big and little and in between,
under slides and play structures and nearby trees)
made you privately giddy, imagining
what words were being exchanged between strangers?
Clothing all dripping and puckered on bodies,
mascara running, no one put together —
you wanted us to be always like this:
disheveled but present,
brought together by the mood of the sky,
willing to look straight at strangers, and laugh
together at the beautiful mess we are.

CHAUTAUQUA, MID-APRIL

I got the impulse
to write a poem,

but all that's left
is laughter, tears

and the mother
of both.

I WANT THAT GOOSE TO BE A TREE

Yesterday I picked up my two-year-old son
from his first day of preschool
drenched in some post-play euphoria
I'd never yet seen,
his tiny eyes opened
to the joyride of finger-paint,
lunch boxes, and songs —

but halfway home his bliss
crested and plunged
into a huge new grief,
which he wailed and howled out
from his carseat behind me.

Look at that huge goose right there!
I offered for distraction
as we drove past the waddling flock.

I want that goose to be a tree!
he cried.

What did you just say?

I want that goose to be a tree!
as sorrowful and stricken
as you can imagine. I felt for him,

of course — his world overwhelmed,
breaking and opening
with the onset of school —

but also, I thought: How creative,
how wonderfully, deeply creative:
I want that goose to be a tree!
Yes, I'd never thought of it,
but that desire is fully available.

And what else? I want this poem
to pour me a glass of red wine!

And,
I want this poem to become a glass of red wine!
I want this to be *your* wine, or whatever beverage
you long for most right now,
and I want this sentence to hand it to you
and watch soulfully while you stop everything
to simply drink,
to drink and know

that your hands can be birds
and your eyes were once telescopes
and the one you dream about
lives locked inside you
in a gesture
you just haven't performed yet.

But that tree could teach it to you,

if you sat and listened long enough,
if you let your heart
suddenly touch and sound
its held wail for the truth
that everything is always changing,
and breaking and opening —

that our drinks together here
are almost done.

ACKNOWLEDGEMENTS

I must begin my thanks to my boys: Lundin (5) and Orion (2). As I write this, I hear you playing upstairs above me. Creating this book has never been about separating from my role and love for you — instead, it has been entangled in and ferociously, tenderly driven by the river of emergence you each erupt in my being. Thank you for inspiring my humbleness and also my greatness, my contact with boundless love and also my grittiest human feelings and limits. Thank you for our stories we are weaving together in this life, and for letting me share some of our stories in these poems as examples of how to be broken down and built up by each other in order to live as love.

Rob, this book is for you. (Ok, you and Kanzeon - haha! - but you are actually not two...) Saying yes to our love was the bright line in my life in which I've been blessed to continuously die into greater love. In a sense, all my quirky behaviors and wild devotion enacted to bring this book to form these past five years have sprung from the immense pleasure of dissolving into and with your great heart again and again. Thank you for giving us all you've got — for being so ridiculously funny and absurd, and so heartbreakingly fearless and compassionate. I worship all of what you are.

Lauren, you are my "art wife." Thank you for being my partner in this crazy, treacherous, exhilarating, intoxicating, sobering practice of courting and expressing creative spirit. All my artistic choices are informed by our love and collaboration. You are so funny and so real and so brilliant. I promise to stay in this with you until the end.

Musho Roshi, thank you for sharing with me the practice that has given me nothing, which is absolutely everything. Thank you for being so generous with your insanely genius powers of perception and skillful means. Thank you for all the sacrifices you have made to give your life to the Buddha, Dharma, and Sangha, and help us weave truly healthy community. I love you and want to honor your awesomeness by serving the practice for the rest of my life. Dragon Heart Sangha, thank you for each of you, your bravery and good will, and for the raw privilege of shaping each other so deeply over time.

Lauren Mitchell Wilkinson, thank you for being the one I go to for feedback on my poems — still, after all these years. It's such a vulnerable thing to receive feedback, and you give it with such elegance and charm. You've been unreasonably generous with your time, attention, and wit, and I'm indebted to you sharing how you see these poems, so they can become more fully realized.

Alex Musat, thank you for your vision and your humble flexibility with me in doing the aesthetic yoga of making this book cover. It's everything I longed for. Jewel Afflerbaugh, thank you for your courage and magic in adventuring to the cover image — what an unforgettable experience of falling into beauty with you! Drummond West, thank you for your wisdom, kindness, and artistry in making films of some of these poems. It is so satisfying to bring them into visual and auditory form!

Fred LaMotte, we've never even met in person, but the first poem of yours I ever read made you my favorite poet of all time. That you've been willing to become my friend over distance since then, and then write the beautiful, crisp, loving foreword for this book has proven what a dear soul you are — thank you. I love you!

To the amazing and many early readers who provided endorsements at the beginning of this book (which are poetry in their own right): thank you for taking time you didn't have and offering gifts to someone less far on the path so that I can convince others to read my book! :) Truly, you all are so generous and I look up to each of you in specific and vivid ways. Thank you so much.

Dad, thank you for loving me with all your heart and always being there for me. Thank you for my life!

Ryan and Lauren, thank you for teaching me how to be funny and strong and heart-centered.

Mom, thank you for teaching me a lifelong love of reading, by osmosis, through watching you nourish yourself with book time every single night. Thank you for the endless love. Thank you for my life!

Thank you to my ancestors who have shown up in some of these stories, and in my dreams and my life, to guide me. Without you, none of this would be. Endless bows of gratitude.

And to you, Reader, thank you from the center of my being. These poems are meant to be your friends, and that can only happen if you let them come close and enter you, and be entered by you. Thank you for being willing to open and rearrange to receive something new. I truly hope it serves you.

ABOUT THE AUTHOR

Brooke McNamara is a poet, performing artist, mother, and monk. She holds a BA in English/ Creative Writing (Poetry) and Dance from Connecticut College, graduating Summa Cum Laude and Phi Beta Kappa, and an MFA in Dance/ Somatic Practice (Yoga) from the University of Colorado, Boulder. Brooke is a lover of adventure and stillness, especially in the territories of creative process, collaborative performance, meditation, and evolution of culture. Her life's work centers around asking beautifully unanswerable questions, and discovering alive answers through wholehearted, creative response.

Brooke has written poems since a young age, and received the Charles B. Palmer Prize through the Academy of American Poets. She is the author of *Feed Your Vow // poems for falling into fullness* (2015), and creator/ instructor for *Write to the Heart of Motherhood*, an online writing course hosted by Next Step Integral for mothers to reclaim their creative spirit and voice in community across the globe. Brooke is also a coach, working one-on-one with clients in creative and contemplative practice.

Brooke has danced professionally for over a decade as a member of *LEVYdance* (San Francisco), *Malashock and*

Dancers (San Diego), and *Kim Olson/ Sweet Edge* (Denver). Since 2010 she has co-directed with Lauren Beale *Eunice Embodiment,* an organization engaging performance, movement education, and *CULTIVATE* creative practice labs and retreats to ignite somatic intelligence, emergent visioning, and collaborative problem-solving for art and life. Brooke has also taught in the Dance Department at CU Boulder and the Yoga Studies department at Naropa University.

Brooke has been a Zen student of Diane Musho Hamilton, Roshi since 2010, and is empowered as a Senior Monk and Dharma Holder. She hosts a weekly practice group and co-hosts a monthly *Day of Zen* as invitations to encounter in community our direct wellspring of wisdom and compassion. Brooke lives in Boulder, CO with her husband, Rob, their sons, Lundin and Orion, and their Bengal kitty, Moxie Joy.

RESOURCES

Brooke McNamara offers online courses and in-person workshops, retreats, and performances in the fields of writing, creative practice, movement, and meditation, as well as one-on-one coaching with emphasis on creative and contemplative practice. To learn more or to contact Brooke, please visit:

www.BrookeMcNamara.com

NOTES

1 Italicized quotation from: Ursula LeGuin, *Always Coming Home* (Berkeley: University of California Press, 1985).

2 Italicized quotation from: Hafiz, *A Year with Hafiz: Daily Contemplations,* trans. Daniel Ladinsky (New York: Penguin Books, 2010).

3 Italicized quotation from: Rob Lloyd Jones, *Space (Look Inside)* (London: Usborne, 2012).

4 Anecdote from: J.F. Martel, *Reclaiming Art in the Age of Artifice* (Berkeley: North Atlantic Books, Evolver Editions: 2015).

5 Italicized quotation from: Billy Collins, *Horoscopes For the Dead: Poems* (New York: Random House Trade Paperbacks, 2012).

www.ingramcontent.com/pod-product-compliance
Lightning Source LLC
Chambersburg PA
CBHW020941090426
42736CB00010B/1214